PSALMS

VOLUME 1

Living Word BIBLE STUDIES

PSALMS

VOLUME 1

Songs Along the Way

KATHLEEN BUSWELL NIELSON

P&R
PUBLISHING
P.O. BOX 817 • PHILLIPSBURG • NEW JERSEY 08865-0817

Printed in the United States of America

ISBN: 978-1-62995-586-5

CONTENTS

CONTENTS

FOREWORD

Today we would call them Christians, but in those days they were sometimes referred to as people who belonged to "the Way" (see Acts 9:2). "The Way" was the way of Jesus, the way he taught his disciples to follow.

We still use the same terminology today to describe our earthly pilgrimage. As we make our own way in the world, we speak of people losing their way, or finding their way, or being on their way. In Christian circles, we also talk about the way of salvation, which can only be found in Jesus. "I *am* the way," he said to his disciples (John 14:6).

This way of speaking did not begin with Jesus but goes all the way back to the Psalms. The very first psalm contrasts "the way of the righteous" with "the way of the wicked." This theme then runs all the way through the Psalter. There are two and only two ways to live: God's way and the way of fallen humanity. Which way will you live? The Psalms help us to choose and then to live our choice.

This study guide is designed to help you make your way through the book of Psalms. The psalms selected cover nearly the full range of material that we find in the Bible's first hymnal. There are psalms of praise and prayer, of suffering and danger, of worship and triumph.

For each kind of psalm, Kathleen Nielson uses her gift for writing clear and compelling questions to help us deal directly with the biblical text. Since she is a poet in her own right, Dr. Nielson has a special sensitivity to the inner workings of biblical poetry. To use her study guide, therefore, is to learn the right way to read, sing, pray, memorize, and meditate on the Psalms.

At the same time, we learn the ways of God. Perhaps more than any other part of the Bible, the book of Psalms gives us a complete overview of God's character. We learn what God loves and hates, what he desires and demands, what he does and plans to do. As John Calvin explained in the preface to his *Commentary on the Psalms*:

> There is no other book in which there is to be found more express and magnificent commendations, both of the unparalleled liberality of God towards his Church, and of all his works; there is no other book in which there is recorded so many deliverances, nor one in which the evidences and experiences of the fatherly providence and solicitude which God exercises towards us, are celebrated with such splendour of diction, and yet with the strictest adherence to truth; in short, there is no other book in which we are more perfectly taught the right manner of praising God, or in which we are more powerfully stirred up to the performance of this religious exercise.

The reason the Psalms tell us so much about God—and help us to praise him so well—is that they were written by God himself. The biblical psalms were written by David, of course, as well as by Asaph and other godly men. But they are also the creative product of God the Holy Spirit.

As we read, therefore, God is helping us find our way to him. He is giving us a lamp to our feet and a light to our path (see Ps. 119:105). My prayer is that as you study these psalms, with the help of this study guide, the Holy Spirit will lead you in "the way everlasting" (Ps. 139:24).

Philip Graham Ryken

A Personal Word
from Kathleen

I began to write these Bible studies for the women in my own church group at College Church in Wheaton, Illinois. Under the leadership of Kent and Barbara Hughes, the church and that Bible study aimed to proclaim without fail the good news of the Word of God. What a joy, in that study and in many since, to see lives changed by the work of the Word, by the Spirit, for the glory of Christ.

In our Bible study group, we were looking for curriculum that would lead us into the meat of the Word and teach us how to take it in, whole Bible books at a time—the way they are given to us in Scripture. Finally, one of our leaders said, "Kathleen—how about if you just write it!" And so began one of the most joyful projects of my life: the writing of studies intended to help unleash the Word of God in people's lives. The writing began during a busy stage of my life—with three lively young boys and always a couple of college English courses to teach—but through that stage and every busy one since, a serious attention to studying the Bible has helped keep me focused, growing, and alive in the deepest ways. The Word of God will do that. If there's life and power in these studies, it is simply the life and power of the Scriptures to which they point. It is ultimately the life and power of the Savior who shines through all the Scriptures from beginning to end. How we need this life, in the midst of every busy and non-busy stage of our lives!

I don't think it is just the English teacher in me that leads me to this conclusion about our basic problem in Bible study these days: we've forgotten how to *read*! We're so used to fast food that we think we should be able to drive by the Scriptures periodically and pick up some easily digestible truths that someone else has wrapped up neatly for us. We've disowned that process of careful reading . . . observing the words . . . seeing the shape of a book and a passage . . . asking questions that take us into the text rather than away from it . . . digging into the Word and letting it speak! Through such a process, guided by the Spirit, the Word of God truly feeds our souls. Here's my prayer: that, by means of these studies, people would be further enabled to read the Scriptures profitably and thereby find life and nourishment in them, as we are each meant to do.

In all the busy stages of life and writing, I have been continually surrounded by pastors, teachers, and family who encourage and help me in this work, and for that I am grateful. The most wonderful guidance and encouragement come from my husband, Niel, whom I thank and for whom I thank God daily.

May God use these studies to lift up Christ and his Word, for his glory!

INTRODUCTION

The way of the Psalms is a well-traveled and blessed way! Not just the psalmists but also God's people throughout many generations have used these words to find their way and to express their prayers and praises to their God along the way. The book of Psalms, often called the Psalter, is the well-worn hymnbook and prayer book of generations of those who have put their faith in the one Lord God.

The title "Psalms" comes from the Greek *psalmoi*, meaning "songs to the accompaniment of a stringed instrument." This was the title used in the days of Jesus. He grew up hearing and learning the psalms sung regularly in temple worship. They were part of the daily devotion and worship of God's people, as they had been already for centuries. The ancient Hebrew title for this collection was *tehillim*, meaning "praise songs." They were gathered and used in various collections as early as the time of Moses, but the final form was probably established by those who served in the rebuilt temple after the exiled Jews had returned to Jerusalem. Thus, the Psalter has often been called "the prayer book for the second temple."

In the Hebrew Scriptures, the scroll of Psalms appeared first in the third division called "the Writings," following "the Law" and "the Prophets." The Writings, then, from the beginning appear in the context of a chosen people who had received God's law through his prophets. The Psalms are the songs and prayers of people called to live in that community of faith and obedience. It is appropriate that the majority of the psalms were written during the years of the monarchy in Israel, for those years, especially under David and Solomon, gave the clearest early picture of what God's kingdom looks like. The Psalms are cries from the kingdom. Even though subsequent generations have learned that God's promised kingdom is larger and greater than the nation of Israel with Jerusalem and its temple at the center, these cries still ring with universal and eternal truth. They celebrate a King like David and Solomon—only much greater. And they point out the path of obedience and blessing for all the subjects of that King (as well as the contrasting path of disobedience and destruction).

Lesson One will provide a more detailed introduction to the book of Psalms. Here let us make three general observations. First, the Psalms clearly show us the ways of God. This collection is certainly not a theological treatise; however, in the course of all the prayers and songs and praises, we cannot fail to grasp the nature and character of the Lord God who is being praised and addressed. His attributes are named and celebrated repeatedly. His ways of dealing with his people are uncovered. The story of his plan and care for Israel (and for his everlasting kingdom) is set forth with overflowing thanksgiving. The inspired seeds of prophecy concerning his redemptive plan, centered in Jesus Christ his Son, are beautifully evident. Even his just punishment of sin, the holy wrath of a holy God, and the final torment of those who reject him emerge with a vividness many find hard to take in. In the Psalms, we can find the whole story of God's dealings with the human creatures he created, from beginning to end. Let us look in the Psalms to find the ways of God.

Second, the Psalms clearly show us the ways of words. What beautiful poetic language is here for us to take in with all our minds, hearts, and imaginations. What true and pleasing rhythms of human experience unfold through the parallel lines of the poetry. What beauty here reflects and celebrates the creativity of God our Maker, who by his word made the world. We are following after our Creator when we follow the power and beauty of these words he inspired. To dig deep into the Psalms, we must dig with relish into their poetic language. Lesson One will provide more specific helps in understanding and appreciating the poetry. Let us look in the Psalms to find the ways of words.

Finally, the Psalms point us to the ways of prayer. These psalms *are* the prayers of God's people, written by them under his inspiration and then used by them for centuries. We make only feeble excuses concerning our inability to pray, when we have such words at our disposal to incorporate into our own prayers. Our increasing unfamiliarity with the words of the Psalter has surely contributed to the struggles and superficialities of our prayers. When the prophet Jonah found himself buried inside a fish in the depths of the sea, he was able to call on Psalms 18, 42, and others, in order to weave together the remarkable prayer of Jonah 2. He had hidden those words in his heart, and they made his prayers rich and fruitful. When Mary found she was with child, carrying the very Son of God, how was she able to give forth such an incredible prayer as we find in the Magnificat (Luke 1:46–55)? She knew the Scriptures. The Psalms especially were in her, and she wove together lines from Psalms 72, 98, 103, and others to pour forth her glorious song to the Lord. The Psalms can teach us how to pray. Let us look in the Psalms to find the ways of prayer.

One last comment on this study, which is the simplest and most uncomplicated one of all my studies: it would be possible to hurry through and be done too quickly with the lessons. I hope you will spend time in the Psalms themselves—musing, marking, meditating, memorizing, and praying. The Psalms will richly reward such time, both presently and in the joys and sorrows of future years.

May the Lord God himself bless this study as we follow the way of the Psalms.

Lesson 1

The Way of the Psalms

This lesson aims to point out the way of the Psalms: to set forth the basic background that will help us dig into the riches of these worship poems. The lesson looks longer than it is! One of the goals is to do a lot of paging through the Psalms in order to become acquainted with the book as a whole before we focus on parts of it.

Day One—The Psalter's Shape and Background

To prepare for a study of the Psalms, let us first see the shape and background of the whole book—which is divided into five separate books. Drawing a parallel with the five books in the law of Moses (often called the Pentateuch), some have called the Psalms "the Pentateuch of David."

1. What do you observe in the concluding verses of each of the five books?

   • Psalm 41:13

   Praise be to the Lord, the God of Israel

1

- Psalm 72:18–20

praise be to his glorious name forever
may the whole earth be filled
with his glory — Amen & Amen

- Psalm 89:52

Praised be the Lord forever
— Amen & Amen

- Psalm 106:48

Praised be to the Lord, the God of Israel
from everlasting to everlasting.
Let all the people say "Amen"!
Praise the Lord

- Psalm 150:6

Let everything that has breath
praise the Lord
Praise the Lord

2. Psalms written by David make up the majority of Books I, II, and V—nearly half the Psalter. Other psalms, both within and without the Psalter, surely were written by him as well. What do we know about David from the following passages?

   a.   I Samuel 16:11–23

   The youngest, glowing in health + handsome. The spirit of the Lord came powerfully upon david. Played the Lyre

   b.   2 Samuel 23:1–7

   Anointed by God, the spirit of God spoke through him.

   c.   I Chronicles 6:31–48

   David put men in charge of the music in the "house of the Lord"

3. What do the superscriptions of various psalms tell us concerning other authors and various contexts of the Psalms? Comment on the introductory text notes of the psalms listed below.

   Helpful facts:

   - *The sons of Korah and Asaph were from the tribe of Levi, in charge of tabernacle, and later temple, care and worship activities.*
   - *The "maskil" and the "miktam" were probably musical compositions used in worship.*
   - *Some of the unidentified words may be names of tunes.*
   - *A "song of ascents" was probably sung in a procession of worshipers walking up to the temple in Jerusalem, the city built high on Mount Zion.*
   - *"Selah," a Hebrew word interspersed throughout the Psalter, may have musical or liturgical significance.*

   a. Psalm 45

   For the director of music. To the tune of "Lilies" of the sons of Korah. A maskil. a wedding song

   b. Psalm 67

   For the director of music. With stringed instruments. A psalm. Asaph

   c. Psalm 70

   For the director of music. Of David. A petition

d.   Psalm 75

In the director of music. To the tune of "Do not destroy". A psalm of Asaph. A song

e.   Psalm 90

A prayer of Moses - the man of God

f.   Psalms 120–134

A song of Ascents

DAY TWO—THE PSALTER'S POETRY

To appreciate the way the Psalms were written, it is necessary to use a translation that presents their poetry in discernible lines. Hebrew poetry's central characteristic is its balancing of lines (or units of thought) in a structure often called parallelism. Most often, two (or sometimes three) "parallel lines" balance together to create meaning. For each of the three generally accepted kinds of parallelism explained below, look through the first several chapters of Psalms and try to find a couple more examples.

1. *Synonymous parallelism*—The second line basically repeats the idea of the first line, in different words (thus adding new shades of meaning).

    a.   Psalm 3:1

Psalms 2: 3, 9

5

b. *Psalms 2:3*

c. *psalms 2:9*
Psalms 4:2

2. *Antithetic parallelism*—The second line presents a contrasting idea.

   a. Psalm 18:27

   b. *Psalms 1:6*

   c. *Psalms 11:5*

3. *Synthetic parallelism*—The second line continues or adds to the meaning of the first.

   a. Psalm 7:10

   b. *Psalms 11:2*

   c. *psalms 12:1*

Even in this exercise, we see that the categories are not always hard and fast. However, the general structure of parallelism appears consistently in the Psalms' poetry. To look for the method and beauty of this structure helps the reader take in this part of God's Word most effectively. How wonderful that, in God's good providence, this parallelism is quite easily captured in translation. The nuances of sound and rhythm are not, but the main characteristic is. We can get close to what the writers—and the Lord!—intended.

Another characteristic of this poetry involves *imagery*, the pictures that lead us to understand God's truth imaginatively and deeply. As we study, let us prepare to note, muse on, and take in the imagery that God inspired in the Psalms.

4. For a start, as we consider imagery, read Psalm 1, chosen to introduce the Psalter. This psalm sets forth two kinds of people, two paths with two different ends, based on two different relationships to God's law. What two main *similes* (comparisons using "like" or "as") picture these two kinds of people?

    A: Like a tree planted by streams of water

    b. Like chaff that wind blows away.

5. Briefly, how do these pictures deepen our understanding of the psalm's meaning?

    Stability & health over lack of permanence and hollowness. Substance vs. shell.

DAY THREE—THE PSALTER'S
BREADTH AND DEPTH

The Psalms reach out and touch just about every imaginable human emotion or expression. In general, from a brief look at the beginning verses of the following psalms, what different kinds of situations and/or expressions can you observe?

- Psalm 4   *Distress*

- Psalm 9   *Thankfulness*
  gladness + rejoicing

- Psalm 13   *Impatience, sorrowful heart*

- Psalm 15   *Truth from the heart*
  generosity

- Psalm 19   *Refreshing the soul*
  fear of the Lord

- Psalm 20   *Distress, shout for joy*

- Psalm 21   *Rejoycing, joy*

- Psalm 30   *Exalt the Lord*
       Praise, rejoice

- Psalm 33   *Joy, praise*

- Psalm 37   *Not fretting, Not being envious*
       Delight in God

- Psalm 51   *Mercy, unfailing love*

- Psalm 59   *Supplications, fear, faith*

- Psalm 67   *Grace, praise, joy*

- Psalm 96   *Rejoicing, praise,*

- Psalm 137   *joy*

And that's only a glimpse! One can understand why both individual believers and worshiping bodies have regularly used the whole progression of psalms to express all their praise, petitions, questionings, thanksgiving, confession, trust, etc., before a God who is worthy of and sufficient for every expression.

DAY FOUR—THE PSALTER'S SAVIOR

From Genesis to Revelation, the Bible presents one unified story about God redeeming a people for himself, through the Lord Jesus Christ. If Jesus is the crux of the story, how does he shine through in the book of Psalms?

For each of the following, read first the verses from the Psalms, then read the New Testament verses, and then summarize briefly how you see Jesus shining through the psalm.

1. Psalm 2:1–6 (cf. John 1:41, 49; 18:36–37; Acts 4:23–27)
   Note: the Greek word Christ *and the Hebrew word* Messiah *both mean literally "the Anointed One."* Rebukes in anger - scoff

   Installed my king on Zion, my holy mountain.

   Anointed one

   Jes' baptism. my son, your father

2. Psalm 2:7–12 (cf. Matt. 3:16–17; Acts 13:32–33; Heb. 1:1–5) Right hand, superior to all - son/father

   Proclaim the Lord's decree - you are my son - nations inheritance. Break w/ rod of iron, clash to pieces. Serve the Lord w/ fear + trembling

3. Psalm 22:1–18 (cf. Matt. 27:32–46)

   Why have you forsaken me? Trust in you

   Divide my clothes. Cast lots

   "Why have you forsaken me."

How amazing to glimpse the ways God inspired the psalmists to write of the Lord Jesus Christ, the Son of God, the one who came as a suffering servant to die for us, the eternal King who reigns on the throne of David, and the one who comes to judge the world. Let us be watchful for Jesus shining through the Psalms as we read and study them.

DAY FIVE—CONCLUSIONS

Having finished this lesson, we have finished only a brief introduction to the Psalms. Having completed the whole study, we will have met only a representative selection of psalms. Let us pray that this study will help lead us into a lifetime of rich communion with God through the Psalms.

To conclude—and to begin!—reread Psalm 1, which stands at the beginning of the Psalter like an open gate inviting us to enter and follow the way of the righteous who delight in God's law—not the way that leads to destruction. The Psalms will help lead us in the right way, following God's law and God's people who have gone before. Having reread Psalm 1, write your own prayer based on it.

The Lord's Glory will settle like a morning dew settles on the high mountains, on those whose heart is pure toward God and who wait on him in patience.

Like the strength of a horse will be that of his loyal servant whose eyes are set on the Lord above and whose lips offer continuous sacrifice for his Glory.

Thoughts and Observations—Psalm 16

Lesson 2 (Psalm 16)

THE WAY OF THE LORD

You make known to me the path of life;
in your presence there is fullness of joy;
at your right hand are pleasures forevermore.

Psalm 16:11

DAY ONE—READ IT

The first day of each lesson will involve prayerful reading, relishing, and observing. First, look up Psalm 16 and read it several times, including an out-loud reading if possible. Pray for understanding and insight, before and as you read. Mark, if you wish, words and sections that stand out to you. Indeed, I encourage you to make all kinds of marks in the text, as this helps to make the text your own. Then write down, on the facing page, your initial thoughts and observations. No matter how basic they are, write down at least five observations concerning the words you read in this psalm.

DAY TWO—THE PRIMARY RELATIONSHIP
(VERSES 1–6)

1. David, the first-person speaker in Psalm 16, begins by addressing God directly. In Psalm 16:1–2, note everything you can about David's relationship to God.

   Note the following terms:

   - *"God"—Hebrew* El, *the name for the Creator*
   - *"LORD"—Hebrew* Yahweh, *the "I am" who reveals himself personally as the one who rules and acts in redemptive history*
   - *"Lord"—Hebrew* Adonay, *meaning "ruler" or "master"*

2. David clearly looks to God first for his refuge and security in this psalm. Where, besides God, do we or other people tend to look for our security these days?

3. According to Psalm 16:3–4, how will such a relationship with the Lord God affect one's relationship with
others—both fellow believers (the "saints" of verse 3)
and nonbelievers (verse 4)?

4. What does Psalm 16:5–6 show about David's perspective
on this relationship with the Lord God and his resulting
perspective on his whole life?

5. In what ways might Psalm 16:5–6 challenge you—in the midst of your present circumstances—to think of the "portion" that has been "allotted" you, and the "inheritance" that you should value? (See also Numbers 18:20 and Lamentations 3:19–26 for further perspective on our richest portion, our most valuable inheritance.)

DAY THREE—RESPONDING TO SUCH A LORD
(VERSES 7–8)

For Psalm 16:7 and then Psalm 16:8, consider the following questions:

1. David is pointing to what aspect(s) of God?

2. What specific responses on David's part do you note?

3. In these verses, what is the relationship of line 1 to line 2?

4. In what ways have you learned (and/or would you like to learn better) the truth of these verses?

DAY FOUR—THE ETERNAL RESULTS OF SUCH A RELATIONSHIP (VERSES 9–11)

1. What results of such a relationship can you observe in Psalm 16:9–11? *Note: "Sheol" in verse 10 means simply "the place of the dead."*

2. How does David, led by the Spirit, prophetically point to Christ in this passage (see Acts 2:22–32 and Acts 13:34–39)?

3. What are the implications, for you personally, of Psalm 16:9–11 and Christ's fulfillment of them?

Day Five—Take It In

1. Think on Jesus, in relation to this psalm. (For further reflection, read Hebrews 12:1-2.) How does Psalm 16 deepen our joy in the God who opens the way of salvation to us through his Son?

2. Each final day of these lessons will ask you to reread the psalm you have studied, and then choose a verse or passage you would like to memorize. Write out the verse or passage and commit it to memory, making it even more a part of your thinking and your prayers. Be ready, if you wish, to tell your group why you picked it. By the end of the study, with regular review, you should have a collection of personal treasures from the Psalms.

Thoughts and Observations—Psalm 32

Lesson 3 (Psalm 32)

THE WAY OF
FORGIVENESS

Blessed is the one whose transgression is forgiven,
whose sin is covered.

Psalm 32:1

DAY ONE—READ IT

First, look up Psalm 32 and read it several times, including an out-loud reading if possible. Pray for understanding and insight, before and as you read. Mark, if you wish, words and sections that stand out to you. Then write down, on the facing page, your initial thoughts and observations. No matter how basic they are, write down at least five observations concerning the words you read in this psalm.

DAY TWO—A CLEAR INTRODUCTION
(VERSES 1–2)

1. After reading Psalm 32:1–2, how would you express in one short statement what this psalm is about?

2. In what four different ways does David describe the process of forgiveness? How does each different phrase add to the meaning?

3. In verses 1–2 and 7–9 of Psalm 51, another penitential psalm of David, how does he further express what forgiveness means?

4. What further connections and clarifications do you find in Romans 3:21–4:8? (Aim not to explicate this passage in detail, but rather to get the main, beautiful thrust of it.)

DAY THREE—BEFORE CONFESSION (VERSES 3–4) AND FINALLY CONFESSION (VERSE 5)

1. In Psalm 32:3–4, in order to illustrate the truth he set forth in his introductory verses, David begins to tell his own story. (Note the change to the first person in verse 3.) What details, phrases, and pictures does he use to communicate his agony of unconfessed sin?

2. What is the relationship between sin and suffering? (See both John 9:1–3 and Psalm 38:1–8.)

3. What mercy do you see in these verses on suffering
   (Ps. 32:3–4)?

4. Psalm 32:5 is the crucial turning point of the whole
   psalm—so simple, clear, and powerful. Write down every
   important word or phrase; why is each so vital?

DAY FOUR—THE RESULTS OF CONFESSION (VERSES 6–11)

1. "Therefore" (v. 6) leads into a beautiful progression of both lessons learned and blessings received through the process of confession. David first would urge the "godly" (those who hear and follow God's voice) to follow his example. What should motivate us to do so, as we listen in on his words to God in Psalm 32:6–7? (Take time to see and savor the picture David paints here.)

2a. God answers David—with what *promises* (v. 8) and what *admonitions* (v. 9)?

b. How do you think these promises (v. 8) and admonitions (v. 9) relate to each other and to the entire psalm?

3. The last two verses conclude, first with a final summary lesson (v. 10) and then with a final call to joy (v. 11). How is each verse a fitting conclusion to the entire psalm? (*Consider: Is the psalm not all about how we can arrive at the blessed rejoicing of the final verse?*)

DAY FIVE—TAKE IT IN

1. Think on Jesus, in relation to this psalm. (For further reflection, read 1 John 1:5-10.) How does Psalm 32 deepen our understanding of God's forgiveness of us through his Son?

2. Reread the psalm you have studied, and then choose a verse or passage you would like to memorize. Write out the verse or passage and commit it to memory, making it even more a part of your thinking and your prayers. Be ready, if you wish, to tell your group why you picked it.

Thoughts and Observations—Psalm 33

Lesson 4 (Psalm 33)

THE WAY OF WORSHIP

Shout for joy in the Lord, O you righteous!
Praise befits the upright.

Psalm 33:1

DAY ONE—READ IT

First, read Psalm 33 several times, including an out-loud reading if possible. Pray for understanding and insight, before and as you read. Mark, if you wish, words and sections that stand out to you. Then write down, on the facing page, your initial thoughts and observations. No matter how basic they are, write down at least five observations concerning the words you read in this psalm.

DAY TWO—GETTING THE SHAPE OF IT

1. First, read verse 1 of Psalm 33. Who are the "righteous" to whom this call is addressed? To answer this question,

look back to Psalm 32 and review the way in which that psalm led us to its similar, closing call to those who are "righteous" and "upright in heart."

2. Psalm 32 moved from the individual "I" to "all" the upright in its final verse. Psalm 33 calls to worship these upright ones who come together as God's holy people. In the following suggested outline, fill in the blanks according to what you find in the verses.

I.   Psalm 33:1–3: Introduction: _____

   _____

II. Psalm 33:4–19: Look at this Lord we worship:

   A. Verses 4–9: He _____

   _____

   B. Verses 10–12: He _____

   _____

   C. Verses 13–19: He _____

   _____

III. Psalm 33:20–22: Concluding response: _____

3. Examine the shape and progression of the opening "call to worship" in Psalm 33:1–3. What various commands are given, and how do they build up beautifully, from the first "shout" to the last "shouts"?

DAY THREE—LOOKING AT THE LORD

1. Psalm 33:4–9 celebrates the word of the Lord. First, his word connects to his *character*. What do you learn about the character of God from the progression of lines in Psalm 33:4–5? *Note: "Steadfast love" in verse 5 is the Hebrew* hesed, *the beautiful and often-used Old Testament word for God's merciful, unfailing love. Look for this word again in this psalm and throughout the Psalms.*

2. God's word connects also to his *creative power*. What phrases in Psalm 33:6–7 make that power even more vivid?

3. How does John 1:1–3 shine light on this passage?

4. How does Psalm 33:8–9 appropriately close this section?

5. Psalm 33:10–12 focuses in a bit, from all of creation to the nations inhabiting that creation.

   a. From each verse's set of synonymous parallel lines, write down the words or groups of words that match. How does this help clarify and deepen the meaning?

   b. What sorts of contrasts or opposites do you notice throughout Psalm 33:10–12?

c. In what way do we as Christians share in the joyful response of Psalm 33:12? (See 1 Peter 2:9.)

DAY FOUR—LOOKING UP TO SEE HIM LOOKING DOWN

1. Psalm 33:13–19 focuses in even more, from the nations in general to the people inhabiting those nations.

a. What is the amazing picture of Psalm 33:13–15, and what details make it even more amazing?

b. What truths does this picture teach us, according to Psalm 33:16–19?

2. How does Psalm 33:20–22 offer a kind of "prayer response" to the entire psalm? Make these verses your response of prayer as well.

DAY FIVE—TAKE IT IN

1. Think on Jesus, in relation to this psalm. (For further reflection, read Hebrews 1:1-4.) How does Psalm 33 deepen our worship of our glorious, redeeming God?

2. Reread the psalm you have studied, and then choose a verse or passage you would like to memorize. Write out the verse or passage and commit it to memory, making it even more a part of your thinking and your prayers. Be ready, if you wish, to tell your group why you picked it.

Thoughts and Observations—Psalm 37

Lesson 5 (Psalm 37)

This Way Versus
the Other

In just a little while, the wicked will be no more;
  though you look carefully at his place, he will not be there.
But the meek shall inherit the land
  and delight themselves in abundant peace.

Psalm 37: 10–11

Day One—Read It

First, read Psalm 37 several times, including an out-loud reading if possible. Pray for understanding and insight, before and as you read. Mark, if you wish, words and sections that stand out to you. Then write down, on the facing page, your initial thoughts and observations. No matter how basic they are, write down at least five observations concerning the words you read in this psalm.

Before reading Psalm 37, note that it is an acrostic poem, with each couple of verses beginning with a successive letter of the Hebrew alphabet. This psalm, then, is ordered more by its external design and less by its own internal progression of ideas. It has clear themes, but it tends to develop them by circling around and around—more like the wisdom literature of Proverbs, for example. Psalm 37 resembles Proverbs also in that it is addressed not to God but to us, showing us the way that leads to life, in contrast with the way that leads to death.

DAY TWO—FRET NOT

1. In Psalm 37:1–11, David speaks directly to followers of the Lord and establishes the main themes of the psalm. What main ideas or themes do you find in these verses?

2. Again in Psalm 37:1–11, list the different *commands* given to followers of the Lord. Then list the different *promises*. How do these lists both challenge and encourage you?

3. What connections do you find to Jesus' words in Matthew 5:5? *Note: God promised a land for the Jews; notice how Jesus shows the depths of that promise for all the people of his kingdom.*

DAY THREE—TWO OPPOSITE PATHS

The remaining verses expound the main themes by contrasting the paths of the "wicked" and the "righteous." For this day's study, carefully examine Psalm 37:12–40 to discover all the contrasts you can find between the wicked and the righteous, in both their present actions and their future ends. Pray through your list of contrasts, asking God to conform you more and more into the image of the only perfectly meek and righteous one, our risen Lord and Savior, Jesus Christ.

DAY FOUR—A MATTER OF PERSPECTIVE

1. This psalm makes sense of the present by looking far into the future. In general, how would you characterize your own attitude and mindset toward the future?

2. Choose and comment briefly on several verses in this psalm that most encourage you to have a "forever" perspective, as opposed to a "right now" perspective.

3. Becoming a "righteous" person with a "forever" perspective is not something we can accomplish ourselves. Look through the psalm and list all the verbs that show what the Lord does. Here is our great reason not to fret, but to trust such a God.

DAY FIVE—TAKE IT IN

1. Think on Jesus, in relation to this psalm. (For further reflection, read Philippians 1:9-11.) How does Psalm 37 deepen our understanding of the righteous life to which God calls us, in Christ?

2. Reread the psalm you have studied, and then choose a verse or passage you would like to memorize. Write out the verse or passage and commit it to memory, making it even more a part of your thinking and your prayers. Be ready, if you wish, to tell your group why you picked it.

Thoughts and Observations—Psalms 42-43

Lesson 6
(Psalms 42-43)

The Way of Tears

Why are you cast down, O my soul,
  and why are you in turmoil within me?
Hope in God; for I shall again praise him,
  my salvation and my God.

Psalm 42:11

Day One—Read It

First, read Psalms 42–43 (which were originally one unified psalm) several times, including an out-loud reading if possible. Pray for understanding and insight, before and as you read. Mark, if you wish, words and sections that stand out to you. Then write down, on the facing page, your initial thoughts and observations. No matter how basic they are, write down at least five observations concerning the words you read in these psalms.

DAY TWO—GETTING THE SHAPE AND CONTEXT

1. What seem to be the identity and the situation (both spiritual and physical) of the speaker as you observe them in Psalm 42? *Note: "Hermon," "Mizar," and "Jordan" may point to places far north of Israel, where the Jordan River originated on the slopes of Mount Hermon—and where the speaker may be for some reason far away from home.*

2. Using the three repeated refrains as markers (study both psalms together as one), how would you describe or outline the three main sections of this poem? What development or progress do you find from beginning to end?

3. Carefully study the refrain itself. What lessons can we learn here about the believer's experience of struggle and turmoil?

Day Three—The Struggle

1. First, in dealing with his downcast and thirsty soul, the psalmist tries remembering (Ps. 42:4, 6). But the remembering precipitates a plunge into the deepest struggle. How do you understand the picture of Psalm 42:7? (See also Jonah 2:3–4.)

    Note: How does the use of the second-person "you" and "your" in Psalm 42:6–7 keep this picture from being one of utter despair? How is the believer's struggle fundamentally different from the unbeliever's despair?

2. Psalm 42:8 is a central verse in the poem, a turning point, a remarkable affirmation that emerges and seems to keep the speaker from drowning in the breakers and waves of struggle. Just what truths are affirmed here in Psalm 42:8? How does Psalm 42:8 answer Psalm 42:1–3?

3. The speaker's troubles do not go away after Psalm 42:8. But what progress do you note in Psalm 42:9–10? Does the refrain in Psalm 42:11 ring any differently at this point than it did the first time?

Day Four—Seeing the Light

Spend this day examining the final section, the prayer of Psalm 43. Write down your thoughts on the following questions: How is Psalm 43 different from the cries of Psalm 42? How has the psalmist's focus changed? What can he affirm, even in the midst of his enemies? What stands out to you as you read the final refrain, which closes this honest, beautiful prayer? Finally, what can you learn from this psalm about praying in the midst of turmoil and struggle?

(Continued from previous page)

DAY FIVE—TAKE IT IN

1. Think on Jesus, in relation to this psalm. (For further reflection, read 1 Corinthians 10:1-4 and 1 Peter 1:3-7.) How do Psalms 42-43 help us put our hope in the One who suffered and died for us?

2. Reread the two psalms you have studied, and then choose a verse or passage you would like to memorize. Write out the verse or passage and commit it to memory, making it even more a part of your thinking and your prayers. Be ready, if you wish, to tell your group why you picked it.

Thoughts and Observations—Psalm 72

Lesson 7 (Psalm 72)

THE WAY OF THE KING

> *Blessed be the LORD, the God of Israel,*
>   *who alone does wondrous things.*
> *Blessed be his glorious name forever;*
>   *may the whole earth be filled with his glory!*
> *Amen and Amen!*
>
> Psalm 72:18–19

DAY ONE—READ IT

First, read Psalm 72 (the final psalm of Book II) several times, including an out-loud reading if possible. Pray for understanding and insight, before and as you read. Mark, if you wish, words and sections that stand out to you. Then write down, on the facing page, your initial thoughts and observations. No matter how basic they are, write down at least five observations concerning the words you read in this psalm.

DAY TWO—WHAT A KING!

Before we look at the broader messianic implications of this magnificent psalm, let us look clearly at the kind of king it

57

celebrates. Psalm 72 was written either by Solomon or for Solomon (or both), and was used by the Jewish people as a blessing and prayer for their kings.

1. First, in Psalm 72:1–7, what characteristics of this king and his kingship are invoked and celebrated?

2a. How does Psalm 72:8–11 show the extent of this king's rule?

b. One might think that only a tyrant could extend his
    rule so effectively; how will this king accomplish it,
    according to Psalm 72:12–14?

3. How might you sum up the blessings prayed for in Psalm
    72:15–17?

DAY THREE—NO EARTHLY KING

We know that David was a godly king, and Solomon was a great one, extending the kingdom to its highest magnificence. But we also know that each of these anointed kings had his weaknesses and faults—and each one passed away, as did the earthly kingdom of the Jewish people. God had promised his people an eternal King, a throne in the line of David that would last forever (see 1 Chron. 17:11–15). When the psalmist wrote Psalm 72, inspired by the Holy Spirit, he wrote about that eternal King, expressing even more than he could understand at the time.

In order to grasp the biblical connections between this psalm and the King of whom it ultimately speaks, read each of the following passages and then write down which verse(s) of Psalm 72 it illumines—and (briefly) *how*. (This rather lengthy exercise will continue into Day Four.)

1. Genesis 12:1–3

2. Isaiah 9:6–7

3. Isaiah 11:1–5

4. Isaiah 61:1–2 (quoted by Jesus with reference to himself in Luke 4:17–21)

5. Jeremiah 23:5–6

DAY FOUR—NO EARTHLY KING (CONTINUED)

6. Zechariah 9:9–10

7. John 3:16–18

8. Romans 3:21–26

9. Revelation 7:9–12; 11:15–18

10. Verses 18–20 close both Psalm 72 and Book II of the Psalter with a beautiful benediction. How do these verses appropriately end the psalm and confirm the messianic significance that we have seen?

DAY FIVE—TAKE IT IN

1. Think on Jesus, in relation to this psalm. (For further reflection, read Hebrews 1:5-9.) How does Psalm 72 inspire you to think of and speak to the Lord Jesus?

2. Reread the psalm you have studied, and then choose a verse or passage you would like to memorize. Write out the verse or passage and commit it to memory, making it even more a part of your thinking and your prayers. Be ready, if you wish, to tell your group why you picked it.

Thoughts and Observations—Psalm 77

Lesson 8 (Psalm 77)

THE WAY OF REMEMBERING

I cry aloud to God,
aloud to God, and he will hear me.

Psalm 77:1

DAY ONE—READ IT

First, read Psalm 77 several times, including an out-loud reading if possible. Pray for understanding and insight, before and as you read. Mark, if you wish, words and sections that stand out to you. Then write down, on the facing page, your initial thoughts and observations. No matter how basic they are, write down at least five observations concerning the words you read in this psalm.

DAY TWO—A DAY OF TROUBLE

In Psalm 77:1–9, we learn much about the speaker. Using specific words and phrases from the text, respond to the following questions:

1. What is the speaker's trouble, and what are his symptoms of that trouble?

2. What positive efforts does he make to deal with his trouble? Why do those efforts seem to fail?

3. As the speaker's "diligent search" (v. 6) brings forth the questions in Psalm 77:7–9, and as those questions are articulated, what can you observe about them?

4. In what ways can you identify with the psalmist's time of trouble, either from your own experience or from the experience of someone close to you? (Explain briefly.)

DAY THREE—A TURNING POINT

1. After the opening, troubled cry, *what changes* in the three "I will" statements of Psalm 77:10–12? What specific details of these verses indicate the change?

2. After the psalmist says he "will," then he *does* it in the remaining verses! What is happening through the progressive lines of Psalm 77:13–15? (For one thing, what pronoun has disappeared, and what pronoun has replaced it?)

3a. What historical event(s) in the life of Israel seems to be behind the wonderful poetry of Psalm 77:16–20? What is the psalmist thinking back on here? (Look through Exodus 15:1–13, watching both for the story and for similar words and phrases.)

b. As opposed to his initial, comfortless sense of an existence cut off from God, what sort of view of the world (and of God) does the speaker portray here in the final section of Psalm 77?

DAY FOUR—RIGHTLY REMEMBERING

1. Certainly it is important for the psalmist to work through the kinds of remembering and questioning that he does in the first part of this psalm. The psalmist of Psalm 42 had to do that as well. They spoke out their troubles, fears, and longings for happier times. But it is vitally important that they did not stop there and so drown in their troubles, fears, and longings. They kept on speaking. And they kept on speaking to the Lord they knew was there. There is one other crucial aspect to what the psalmist does here: he remembers in a different way, starting in Psalm 77:10. Read the following verses and consider this question: How should the stories and truths of the Scriptures invade and transform our thoughts and even our memories?

   - Deuteronomy 4:9–14
   - Nehemiah 9:16–17
   - Psalm 78:1–8
   - 1 Corinthians 11:23–26

2. Consider one more time just where the psalmist has come in the progress of this psalm. Look at his solitary, first-person cry in Psalm 77:1–3, and then contrast that with his affirmation in the last two verses: What do you observe?

For meditation: Do you tend to view yourself more as an individual reaching for God, or more as part of his "people," his "flock," led by the Lord together through his Word and through the spiritual leaders he provides?

DAY FIVE—TAKE IT IN

1. Think on Jesus, in relation to this psalm. (For further reflection, read Luke 1:68-75.) How does Psalm 77 help us, in our times of trouble, to remember what God has done for us through his Son?

2. Reread the psalm you have studied, and then choose a verse or passage you would like to memorize. Write out the verse or passage and commit it to memory, making it even more a part of your thinking and your prayers. Be ready, if you wish, to tell your group why you picked it.

Thoughts and Observations—Psalm 98

Lesson 9 (Psalm 98)

THE WAY OF PRAISE

Oh sing to the LORD a new song,
for he has done marvelous things!

Psalm 98:1

DAY ONE—READ IT

First, read Psalm 98 several times, including an out-loud reading if possible. Pray for understanding and insight, before and as you read. Mark, if you wish, words and sections that stand out to you. Then write down, on the facing page, your initial thoughts and observations. No matter how basic they are, write down at least five observations concerning the words you read in this psalm.

DAY TWO—SING A NEW SONG!

1. As you study Psalm 98:1–3, what main work of God is celebrated (mentioned in each verse)? What different

aspects of this work (and of the one who does it) does the psalmist particularly highlight?

2. Scripture is the whole story of salvation, of God's deliverance—his *saving* of a death-doomed people. That salvation was from the beginning found in Jesus Christ, who was promised; who then came and died for the sins of sinful people; who rose again, conquering death; *and* who will come again to judge and to reign forever—as we shall anticipate at the end of Psalm 98. What this psalm focuses on at its start is the *joy* of this salvation, a consistent theme throughout Scripture. How do the following verses carry and deepen this theme?

• Isaiah 12:2–3

• Isaiah 61:10

• Habakkuk 3:17–18

3. Why is the song of salvation a "new song," as Psalm 98:1 puts it? (See also Psalm 40:1–3.)

DAY THREE—WE RESPOND TO
THE GOD OF OUR SALVATION

1. What different commands do you find in Psalm 98:4–6? What would you say is the theme of this section? *Note: The Hebrew verb for "sing praises" is the root for the word* psalm.

2. List all the different sounds you hear in these verses. These were sounds the Jews would have heard either in temple celebrations or in the royal welcome of a king; how is this psalm's celebration both similar to and different from these?

3. How does this psalm, so far, instruct us concerning the nature of praise and worship?

DAY FOUR—THE RESPONSE OF PRAISE EXPANDS

1. In the final section, joyful praise stretches out through all creation. Relish the poetry of Psalm 98:7–8. What details of language and imagery stand out to you in these two sets of parallel lines?

2. What is the reason given in Psalm 98:9 for the exultation of the created order? How do the details given connect to the rest of the psalm?

3. Jesus Christ *has* come, and yet we can still participate in the cry of this psalm, because, according to Scripture, he *will come again* finally to judge, to make a new heaven and earth, and to reign forever. In what ways do the following verses echo and deepen the theme of all creation longing to be made right and new in the end, when Jesus comes?

    •   Psalm 96:11–13

    •   Isaiah 55:12–13

• Romans 8:18–25

DAY FIVE—TAKE IT IN

1. Think on Jesus, in relation to this psalm. (For further reflection, read Revelation 5:9-14.) How does Psalm 98 help enlarge the "new song" to our Lord Jesus?

2. Reread the psalm you have studied, and then choose a verse or passage you would like to memorize. Write out the verse or passage and commit it to memory, making it even more a part of your thinking and your prayers. Be ready, if you wish, to tell your group why you picked it.

Thoughts and Observations—Psalm 103

Lesson 10 (Psalm 103)

THE WAY OF BLESSING

Bless the LORD, *O my soul,*
   and all that is within me,
   bless his holy name!
Bless the LORD, *O my soul,*
   and forget not all his benefits. . . .

Psalm 103:1–2

DAY ONE—READ IT

First, read Psalm 103 several times, including an out-loud reading if possible. Pray for understanding and insight, before and as you read. Mark, if you wish, words and sections that stand out to you. Then write down, on the facing page, your initial thoughts and observations. No matter how basic they are, write down at least five observations concerning the words you read in this psalm.

DAY TWO—BLESS THE LORD

1. There is no better way to get at this psalm than to start
   with its "bookends": Psalm 103:1–2 and Psalm 103:20–22.
   Comment on these verses as carefully and specifically as
   possible.

   a. How does Psalm 103:1–2 establish the theme and
      the tone of the psalm?

   b. How does Psalm 103:1–2 imply a kind of corrective
      to some of our natural tendencies?

   c. How does Psalm 103:20–22 both reemphasize and
      enlarge the theme?

2. Psalm 103:2 overflows into Psalm 103:3, as it begins to enumerate "all his benefits." List all the verbs in Psalm 103:3–5 that tell us what God does. How do you respond?

3. What about that eagle in Psalm 103:5? How does such a picture express what God does for us? (See also Isaiah 40:30–31.)

DAY THREE—WHAT A MERCIFUL LORD

1. Carefully read Psalm 103:6–12 and then review Exodus 33:18–34:9, which happens right after the Israelites have sinned by creating and worshiping a golden calf. Moses intercedes for them, and God has mercy. He even reveals himself further to Moses, in all his glory, speaking the words of Psalm 103:8. What aspects of the Lord's mercy does Psalm 103:6–12 reveal to you?

2. How do the details and the pictures of Psalm 103:11–12 further deepen our wonder and grasp of God's merciful forgiveness?

3. Why do you think we tend to take for granted the fact that God does not deal with us as our sins deserve? Why do we so easily "forget this benefit"? Reread Psalm 103:6–12, thanking God that he forgives sin and "works righteousness" (v. 6) for us—ultimately through Jesus Christ, who became sin for us, even though he knew no sin, in order that in him we might become the righteousness of God (2 Cor. 5:21).

DAY FOUR—WHAT A COMPASSIONATE LORD AND EVERLASTING KING!

1. Psalm 103:13–19 has two sides. The first shows God looking down with compassion on the fleeting lives of his children. How do the vivid pictures in Psalm 103:13–16 communicate both the compassion and the fleetingness?

2. The second side of Psalm 103:13–19 does not show God looking down with compassion; it shows his children looking up with the proper kind of fear. What kind of God do we find in Psalm 103:17–19, and what is our rightful response to him?

3. In what ways might Psalm 103:19 surprise you as the culmination of this whole psalm? How does this verse provide a fitting climax? How does it prepare us for the concluding verses of blessing?

4. How might this psalm affect your prayers?

DAY FIVE—TAKE IT IN

1. Think on Jesus, in relation to this psalm. (For further reflection, read Ephesians 1:3-10.) How does Psalm 103 beautifully unfold the richness of God's blessings given to us in Christ?

2. Reread the psalm you have studied, and then choose a verse or passage you would like to memorize. Write out the verse or passage and commit it to memory, making it even more a part of your thinking and your prayers. Be ready, if you wish, to tell your group why you picked it.

Thoughts and Observations—Psalm 119

Lesson 11 (Psalm 119)

THE WAY OF THE WORD

In the way of your testimonies I delight
as much as in all riches.

Psalm 119:14

DAY ONE—READ IT

Before you read Psalm 119, note that this psalm is another acrostic poem, like Psalm 37—only here each Hebrew letter introduces eight verses in a row (a stanza). The twenty-two stanzas, following as they do an exterior stylistic structure rather than a purely internal logic, wind around a variety of themes, all having to do with the main theme of God's word. For Day One, read the first three stanzas (vv. 1–24), which provide a good introduction to the psalm, its main theme, and its various minor themes. For the remainder of the lesson, we will refer to the complete text of Psalm 119.

First, read the initial three stanzas several times, including an out-loud reading if possible. Pray for understanding and insight, before and as you read. Mark, if you wish, words and sections that stand out to you. Then write down, on the facing page, your initial thoughts and observations. No matter how basic they are, write down at least five observations about this portion of the psalm.

DAY TWO—ENTERING INTO THE PRAYER

1. How does Psalm 119:1–3 seem to be set apart from the rest of the psalm, as a kind of introduction?

2. Psalm 119:4 begins a long, personal, beautiful prayer addressed directly to the Lord—a prayer with a topic: God's word. Read through five stanzas or more of the psalm and write down all the different names the psalmist uses for God's word. Why do you think he uses all these different terms?

3. Through this prayer concerning God's word, the psalmist is not aiming just to learn or know it really well, is he? What is he after, through his prayers about the word (see Ps. 119:2, 10–12, 57, 62, 135)?

4. As we study this psalm, let us look for ways in which it can teach us to pray. There is hardly another psalm more beautiful to pray through out loud. What have you learned or been reminded of, even so far, that might affect the way you pray?

DAY THREE—ATTITUDES AND ACTIONS

Spend this day's study again reading through at least five stanzas, observing and writing down various *attitudes* and *actions* of the psalmist in relation to God's word. As you finish, reread what you have written and write a short response.

DAY FOUR—ASKING ACCORDING TO THE WORD

Choose one stanza on which to focus, looking for *what* the psalmist asks of God, and *why*. Psalm 119:33–40 offers one of the most beautiful examples of requests and motives combined— but choose any stanza that you find fruitful for this question. In conclusion, spend a few moments praying according to the verses you chose.

(Continued from previous page)

DAY FIVE—TAKE IT IN

1. Think on Jesus, in relation to this psalm. (For further reflection, read John 1:1-5, 14-18.) How does Psalm 119 help lead us to see and love the Lord Jesus?

2. Look again through (or reread!) the psalm you have studied, and then choose a verse or passage you would like to memorize. Write out the verse or passage and commit it to memory, making it even more a part of your thinking and your prayers. Be ready, if you wish, to tell your group why you picked it.

Comments On Psalm 121

Lesson 12 (Psalms 121, 123, 126, 131, 150)

The Way Up: Four Psalms of Ascent, and One of Arrival!

Day One—Psalm 121

The final lesson of this study departs from the usual format, taking one short psalm from Book V for each day. The first four are songs of ascent, probably sung in a procession of Jewish worshipers walking up toward the temple in Jerusalem, the city built high on Mount Zion. These songs sometimes communicate the perspective of looking up at Mount Zion, up toward the temple. Reading them, we might gain a better sense of living our lives as a blessed journey toward God's full presence—sometimes a hard journey, sometimes a joyful one, but always a journey made with our eyes lifted toward our destination. Each song of ascent is simple and moving, with one vivid, central idea. For each of the four songs of ascent, beginning this day with Psalm 121, look up the psalm and read it carefully and prayerfully, and then comment on these three questions:

1. What is the central idea that shines forth in this psalm?

2. What vivid words and images help communicate that central idea, and how?

3. What would you like to take away from this psalm?

Comments on today's psalm can be written on the facing page.

DAY TWO—PSALM 123

1. What is the central idea that shines forth in this psalm?

2. What vivid words and images help communicate that central idea, and how?

3. What would you like to take away from this psalm?

DAY THREE—PSALM 126

1. What is the central idea that shines forth in this psalm?

2. What vivid words and images help communicate that central idea, and how?

3. What would you like to take away from this psalm?

DAY FOUR—PSALM 131

1. What is the central idea that shines forth in this psalm?

2. What vivid words and images help communicate that central idea, and how?

3. What would you like to take away from this psalm?

Day Five—A Final Outburst of Praise!

1. Think on Jesus, in relation to these four psalms of ascent. (For further meditation, read Colossians 3:1-4; Hebrews 10:19-25.) How do these psalms of ascent, in all their longing and hope, point us to the Lord Jesus?

2. We will end with the last psalm in the Psalter! Read (out loud if at all possible) and joyfully pray Psalm 150. This psalm offers not only a benediction closing Book V, but also a final benediction to the whole book of Psalms; a benediction made of pure, joyful praise to the Lord. Try to hear the climax of sounding praise with which the Psalter closes. This psalm makes us feel as if we have arrived "in the sanctuary" after that journey of ascents.

Praise God: we *have* arrived, in our eternal and risen Lord Jesus Christ, in whom all the promises of God are "Yes" (2 Cor. 1:20).

3. Finally, review the verses you have chosen to memorize (for Day Five of each lesson). Have you indeed created a collection of personal treasures from the book of Psalms? Perhaps you will take with you from this study a desire to "hide in your heart" more passages from Psalms—maybe even whole psalms at a time. May this rich book of prayer and praise increasingly bless and nurture us every step of the way until we arrive in the heavenly Zion.

Notes for Leaders

What a privilege it is to lead a group in studying the Word of God! Following are six principles offered to help guide you as you lead.

1. The Primacy of the Biblical Text

If you forget all the other principles, I encourage you to hold on to this one! The Bible is God speaking to us, through his inspired Word—living and active and sharper than a two-edged sword. As leaders, we aim to point people as effectively as possible into this Word. We can trust the Bible to do all that God intends in the lives of those studying with us.

This means that the job of a leader is to direct the conversation of a group constantly back into the text. If you "get stuck," usually the best thing to say is: "Let's go back to the text and read it again. . . ." The questions in this study aim to lead people into the text, rather than into a swirl of personal opinions about the topics of the text; therefore, depending on the questions should help. Personal opinions and experiences will often enrich your group's interactions; however, many Bible studies these days have moved almost exclusively into the realm of "What does this mean to me?" rather than first trying to get straight on "What does this mean?"

We'll never understand the text perfectly, but we can stand on one of the great principles of the Reformation: the *perspicuity* of Scripture. This simply means *understandability*. God made us word-creatures, in his image, and he gave us a Word that he wants us to understand more and more, with careful reading and study, and shared counsel and prayer.

The primacy of the text implies less of a dependence on commentaries and answer guides than often has been the case. I do not offer answers to the questions, because the answers are in the biblical text, and we desperately need to learn how to dig in and find them. When individuals articulate what they find for themselves (leaders included!), they have learned more, with each of their answers, about studying God's Word. These competencies are then transferable and applicable in every other study of the Bible. Without a set of answers, a leader will not be an "answer person," but rather a fellow searcher of the Scriptures.

Helps *are* helpful in the right place! It is good to keep at hand a Bible dictionary of some kind. The lessons themselves actually offer context and help with the questions as they are asked. A few commentaries are listed in the "Notes on Translations and Study Helps," and these can give further guidance after one has spent good time with the text itself. I place great importance as well on the help of leaders and teachers in one's church, which leads us into the second principle.

2. THE CONTEXT OF THE CHURCH

As Christians, we have a new identity: we are part of the body of Christ. According to the New Testament, that body is clearly meant to live and work in local bodies, local churches. The ideal context for Bible study is within a church body—one that is reaching out in all directions to the people around it. (Bible studies can be the best places for evangelism!) I realize that these studies will be used in all kinds of ways and places; but whatever the context, I would hope that the group leaders have a layer of solid church leaders around them, people to whom they can go with questions and concerns as they study the Scriptures. When a leader doesn't know the answer to a question that arises, it's really OK to say, "I don't know. But I'll be happy to try to find out." Then that leader can go to pastors and teachers, as well as to commentaries, to learn more.

The church context has many ramifications for Bible study. For example, when a visitor attends a study and comes to know the Lord, the visitor—and his or her family—can be plugged into the context of the church. For another example, what happens in a Bible study often can be integrated with other courses of study within the church, and even with the preaching, so that the whole body learns and grows together. This depends, of course, on the connection of those leading the study with those leading the church—a connection that I have found to be most fruitful and encouraging.

3. THE IMPORTANCE OF PLANNING AND THINKING AHEAD

How many of us have experienced the rush to get to Bible study on time . . . or have jumped in without thinking through what will happen during the precious minutes of group interaction . . . or have felt out of control as we've made our way through a quarter of the questions and used up three-quarters of the time!

It is crucial, after having worked through the lesson yourself, to think it through from the perspective of leading the discussion. How will you open the session, giving perhaps a nutshell statement of the main theme and the central goals for the day? (Each lesson offers a brief introduction that will help with the opening.) Which questions do you not want to miss discussing, and which ones could you quickly summarize or even skip? How much time would you like to allot for the different sections of the study?

If you're leading a group by yourself, you will need to prepare extra carefully—and that can be done! If you're part of a larger study, perhaps with multiple small groups, it's helpful for the various group leaders to meet together and to help each other with the planning. Often, a group of leaders meets early on the morning of a study, in order to help the others with the fruit of their study, plan the group time, and pray—which leads into the fourth principle.

4. The Crucial Role of Prayer

If these words we're studying are truly the inspired Word of God, then how much we need to ask for his Spirit's help and guidance as we study his revelation! This is a prayer found often in Scripture itself, and a prayer God evidently loves to answer: that he would give us understanding of his truth, according to his Word. I encourage you as a leader to pray before and as you work through the lesson, to encourage those in your group to do the same, to model this kind of prayer as you lead the group time, to pray for your group members by name throughout the week, and to ask one or two "prayer warriors" in your life to pray for you as you lead.

5. The Sensitive Art of Leading

Whole manuals, of course, have been written on this subject! Actually, the four principles preceding this one may be most fundamental in cultivating your group leadership ability. Again, I encourage you to consider yourself not as a person with all the right answers, but rather as one who studies along with the people in your group—and who then facilitates the group members' discussion of all they have discovered in the Scriptures.

There is always a tension between pouring out the wisdom of all your own preparation and knowledge, on the one hand,

and encouraging those in your group to relish and share all they have learned, on the other. I advise leaders to lean more heavily toward the latter, reserving the former to steer gently and wisely through a well-planned group discussion. What we're trying to accomplish is not to cement our own roles as leaders, but to participate in God's work of raising up mature Christians who know how to study and understand the Word—and who will themselves become equipped to lead.

With specific issues in group leading—such as encouraging everybody to talk, or handling one who talks too much—I encourage you to seek the counsel of one with experience in leading groups. There is no better help than the mentoring and prayerful support of a wise person who has been there! That's even better than the best "how-to" manual. If you have a number of group leaders, perhaps you will invite an experienced group leader to come and conduct a practical session on how to lead.

Remember: the default move is, "Back to the text!"

6. The Power of the Scriptures to Delight

Finally, in the midst of it all, let us not forget to delight together in the Scriptures! We should be serious but not joyless! In fact, we as leaders should model for our groups a growing and satisfying delight in the Word of God—as we notice its beauty, stop to linger over a lovely word or phrase, enjoy the poetry, appreciate the shape of a passage from beginning to end, laugh at a touch of irony or an image that hits home, wonder over a truth that pierces the soul.

May we share and spread the response of Jeremiah, who said:

> Your words were found, and I ate them,
>   and your words became to me a joy
>   and the delight of my heart. (Jer. 15:16)

Notes on Translations and Study Helps

This study can be done with any reliable translation of the Bible, although I do recommend the English Standard Version for its essentially literal but beautifully readable translation of the original languages. In preparing this study, I have used and quoted from the English Standard Version, published by Crossway Bibles in Wheaton, Illinois. Whichever additional translation you might choose, it will be most helpful if it consistently reflects the parallel structure of the original Hebrew poetry (see Lesson One).

These lessons are designed to be completed with only the Bible open in front of you. The point is to grapple with the text, not with what others have said about the text. The goal is to know, increasingly, the joy and reward of digging into the Scriptures, God's breathed-out words which are not only able to make us wise for salvation through faith in Christ Jesus but also profitable for teaching, reproof, correction, and training in righteousness, so that each of us may be competent, equipped for every good work (2 Tim. 3:15–17). To help you "dig in," basic and helpful contexts and comments are given throughout the lessons. I have used and learned from the following books in my own study and preparation; you may find sources such as these helpful at some point.

GENERAL HANDBOOKS:

The Crossway Comprehensive Concordance of the Holy Bible: English Standard Version. Compiled by William D. Mounce. Wheaton: Crossway Books, 2002. (Other concordances are also available, from various publishers and for different translations.)

The Illustrated Bible Dictionary. 4 vols. Wheaton: Tyndale House Publishers, 1980. (*The Zondervan Pictorial Encyclopedia of the Bible* is similarly helpful.)

Ryken, Leland, James Wilhoit, and Tremper Longman III, eds. *Dictionary of Biblical Imagery*. Downers Grove, IL: InterVarsity Press, 1998.

Ryken, Leland, Philip Ryken, and James Wilhoit. *Ryken's Bible Handbook*. Wheaton, IL: Tyndale House Publishers, 2005.

Vine's Complete Expository Dictionary of Old and New Testament Words. Nashville: Thomas Nelson, 1984.

COMMENTARIES:

Boice, James Montgomery. *Psalms.* 3 vols. Grand Rapids: Baker Books, 1994.

Bridges, Charles. *An Exposition of Psalm 119.* Carlisle, PA: Banner of Truth Trust, 1995 (first published 1827).

Kidner, Derek. *Psalms.* Tyndale Old Testament Commentary. 2 vols. London: Inter-Varsity Press, 1973–1975.

Knight, George A. F. *Psalms.* Daily Study Bible Series Commentary. 2 vols. Philadelphia: Westminster, 1982–1983.

Lewis, C. S. *Reflections on the Psalms.* New York: Harcourt, Brace & World, 1958.

Kathleen Nielson (MA, PhD in literature, Vanderbilt University) has taught in the English departments at Vanderbilt University, Bethel College (Minnesota), and Wheaton College. She is the author of numerous Bible studies, the book *Bible Study: Following the Ways of the Word*, and various articles and poems. Kathleen has directed and taught women's Bible studies at several churches and speaks extensively at conferences and retreats. She serves as advisor and editor for The Gospel Coalition and was its director of women's initiatives from 2010–2017. She is also on the board of directors of The Charles Simeon Trust.

Kathleen and her husband Niel have three sons, two beautiful daughters-in-law, and a growing number of grandchildren!

ALSO BY KATHLEEN BUSWELL NIELSON

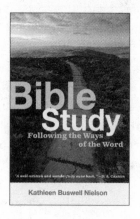

"Dissatisfied with leaving Bible study to the professionals while the rest of us are mere recipients of their work, Kathleen Nielson wants all Christians to be involved in thoughtful and faithful Bible study—and tells us how to do it."

—D. A. CARSON, Research Professor of New Testament, Trinity Evangelical Divinity School

"Nielson gives her readers a fresh and innovative, yet solid and God-glorifying approach to unlocking the truths of Scripture ... by reading God's words in order to ask what God is saying and how one should respond to him."

—DOROTHY PATTERSON, General Editor, *The Woman's Study Bible*

"The book cannot be better than it is ... it covers all the right topics in exactly the right order! For people who teach the Bible— or who aspire to teach it—this book will be the gold standard for knowing how to do it right."

—LELAND RYKEN, Professor of English, Wheaton College